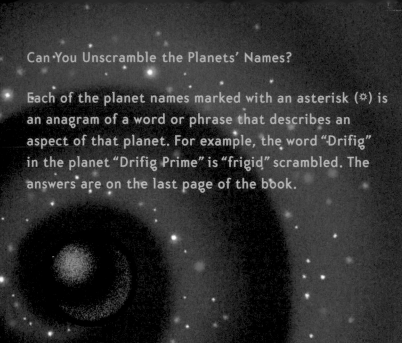

Can You Unscramble the Planets' Names?

Each of the planet names marked with an asterisk (✻) is an anagram of a word or phrase that describes an aspect of that planet. For example, the word "Drifig" in the planet "Drifig Prime" is "frigid" scrambled. The answers are on the last page of the book.

For Janet, who believed in this book. —Jack Prelutsky

THE SWAMPS OF SLEETHE

poems from beyond the solar system

by jack prelutsky

illustrated by jimmy pickering

alfred a. knopf
new york

THE SWAMPS OF SLEETHE

On sweltering Sleethe, in swamps aseethe,
Malignant beings thrive,
Abhorrent things that need not breathe,
And yet are quite alive.
Within a foul and festering broth,
These mucid horrors ooze.
As gluey fluids fume and froth,
They hold their rendezvous.

And there through time beyond all time,
Suffused with rage and hate,
They've been in that miasmic slime
Too vile to contemplate.
If by some trick of fate you find
This world wherein they lurk,
Then you shall leave your bones behind
Beneath the Sleethian murk.

SLEETHE—rhymes with *breathe*

THE COLD OF DRIFIG* PRIME

No human being can survive
The cold of Drifig Prime,
For there your body freezes
In abbreviated time.
You soon lose all sensation
In your fingers and your feet,
You feel your heart grow weaker,
Then completely cease to beat.

Your bones are icy splinters,
And your blood solidifies.
Your flesh becomes so frigid
It begins to crystallize.
Your eyes are sightless marbles,
And your brain, turned brittle, splits.
You topple onto Drifig Prime,
And shatter into bits.

DRIH-fig PRIME

THE FORESTS OF FESSTOR*

The forests of Fesstor are fragrant,
And the forests of Fesstor are wild,
But the forests of Fesstor are not what they seem,
Beware of those forests, dear child.
Every bush, every bud, every blossom
Is filled with malevolent will.
The prettiest mosses may poison,
The loveliest lichens may kill.

The delicate twigs are deceitful,
And pierce you with torturous spines.
There is pain in the touch of the branches,
There is fire in the whip of the vines.
There are treacherous grasses to catch you,
Coarse roots that can snatch you away.
There are metal-sharp petals to scratch you,
There is peril wherever you stray.

The leaves softly weave evil garlands
To snare you and choke off your breath.
The trees may crash downward and crush you—
There is naught in the forests but death.
Yes, the forests of Fesstor are fragrant,
And the forests of Fesstor are wild,
But the forests of Fesstor are not what they seem,
Beware of those forests, dear child.

FESS-tore

THE GLOBULINGS OF WOLVAR SPROD

The globulings of Wolvar Sprod,
The moment that you land,
Will capture you for reasons
That you cannot understand.

They'll place you on a pedestal,
And endlessly revolve you,
Until they weary of their sport—
And that's when they'll dissolve you.

GLOB-you-lings of WOOL-var SPRAHD

THE BUGS OF GUB*

The bugs of Gub, no two alike,
Are all designed to swiftly strike.
They'll swarm upon your tender skin,
And gnaw your nose, and chomp your chin.

They're merciless, relentless things,
With dreadful venom in their stings.
They'll land on you with jaws agape,
And soon you'll find there's no escape.

The bugs of Gub will bite and chew
Until there's nothing left of you,
Not even the remotest trace
On Gub, your final resting place.

GUB—rhymes with *rub*

THE DEMON BIRDS OF LONITHOR

The demon birds of Lonithor
Have seven sets of wings.
They never sing a single song,
But they do *other* things.
They soar above their planet
On perennial patrol—
To feast on otherworlders
Is their all-consuming goal.

They're larger than the largest beast
That you have ever seen.
Their monstrous beaks are scimitars,
Their sight is deadly keen.
Their heads are red as rubies,
And their bodies black as night.
A flock in full formation
Is a terrifying sight.

Their hunger is insatiable,
And will not be denied.
If ever they espy you,
There is nowhere you can hide.
You're utterly defenseless
When they plummet from above.
Before you know what's happening,
You lose the life you love.

They'll grasp you in a fierce embrace,
And carry you away,
Then tear you with their talons
That eviscerate their prey.
And when they've disemboweled you,
They'll pick apart your face. . . .
Don't ever visit Lonithor
When you're in outer space.

LAH-nuh-thore

AS SOON AS YOU'RE ON SWOLE

As soon as you're on Swole
You feel a sense of emptiness,
An overwhelming sadness
Words are useless to express.
Despite the fields of flowers
Wafting perfume in the air,
You're steeped in unremitting gloom
And fathomless despair.

As soon as you're on Swole
You shed a sea of salty tears.
You wish that you could shut your eyes
And sleep a thousand years.
You cannot stem the misery
That seeps into your soul—
You forfeit laughter in your life
As soon as you're on Swole.

SWOLE—rhymes with *hole*

THERE'S SOMETHING ON SKREBER

There's something on Skreber
That drives you to laughter,
You laugh and you laugh
Without reason or sense.
You throw back your head
And you laugh unabated,
You bend over double,
The pain is intense.

There's nothing that's funny,
And yet you keep laughing,
You laugh yourself crazy,
You laugh yourself blue.
You laugh till you wish
You'd expire of laughter,
And in that same second,
You mercifully do.

SKRAY-burr

ON GROB

When you're on Grob, you undergo
A cataclysmic change
Beyond your understanding,
And unconscionably strange.
Your ankles ache and tremble,
And you don't like how that feels.
You glance down at your feet, and find
They're now a pair of wheels.

Your innards turn to girders,
Cams and pulleys, cogs and gears.
Your arms are lengthy tentacles
That end in hooks and shears.
Your neck is ringed with skewers,
You have quills on either knee,
And a laser-guided cannon
Where your belly used to be.

You feel your body altering
In every single cell.
Your torso is enveloped
By an armor-plated shell.
Your facial features melt away
Until they disappear,
Your head becomes a steely,
Slightly elongated sphere.

No longer can you speak a word,
You only click and hiss.
You've reached the final stages
Of your metamorphosis.
The person that you were
Is now irrevocably gone—
You remain on Grob forever,
A bizarre automaton.

GROB—rhymes with *knob*

THE BEHOLDER IN THE SILENCE

On a planet gray and airless
At the universe's rim,
Where the night is everlasting
And the stars are ever dim,
The Beholder in the Silence
Waits immobile, hushed, and grim.

On that world of desolation
Where no mortal being has stepped,
The Beholder in the Silence
Has its timeless vigil kept,
And for eons past all measure,
It has neither stirred nor slept.

—

The Beholder in the Silence,
With its one unblinking eye,
Stares into the boundless cosmos
Far beyond its sunless sky.
We cannot divine the meaning,
But can only wonder why.

The Beholder in the Silence
Keeps its vigil all alone
For a reason and a purpose
That forever stays unknown,
On that chill and nameless planet
Where no wind has ever blown.

ON FABLED GAZOOK

On fabled Gazook
You'll be showered with praise,
The toast and delight
Of the local gourmets.

The cooks of Gazook
Will reduce you to powder,
And use you to flavor
Their savory chowder.

guh-ZOOK

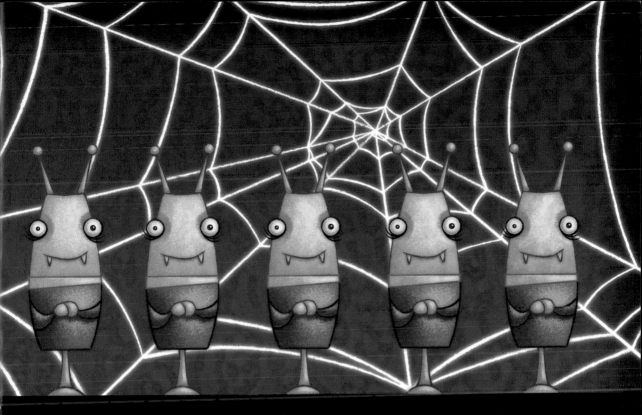

THE MONOPODS OF OGDOFOD ☼

The monopods of Ogdofod,
Although they're small and neat,
Are not the sort of beings
That you ever want to meet.

The monopods of Ogdofod
Will snare you in their nets,
Then process you and package you
To feed their hungry pets.

THE WATERS OF WONTHOO

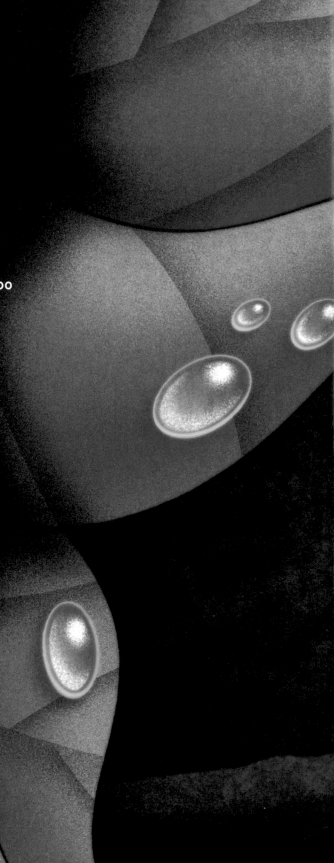

The waters of Wonthoo are sweet,
And yet unfit to drink,
For if you take a single sip,
You're guaranteed to shrink.
It happens very rapidly,
And cannot be reversed,
And soon you'll rue that on Wonthoo
You tried to slake your thirst.

Before a minute's time has passed,
You're stunned to realize
You've shrunk to but a quarter
Of your customary size.
You continue to diminish,
And in one surprising spurt,
You're significantly smaller
Than a button on your shirt.

You soon are microscopic,
As in seconds you become
The size of an amoeba
Or a paramecium.
You finally evaporate,
Much like a drop of dew,
And all because you dared to drink
The waters of Wonthoo.

one-THOO

ON SARBRO*

On Sarbro you quickly discover
That world takes a terrible toll,
As you undergo a mutation
Completely beyond your control.
You grow over twenty feet taller,
The girth of your body expands,
Your every last muscle is useless,
And cannot obey your commands.

Your trunk becomes harder and rougher
As branches sprout out of your head.
Your hair disappears in an instant—
You've leaves by the thousands instead.
No more can you wander the cosmos,
No more will you ever run free,
For now you are rooted on Sarbro,
To live out your life as a tree.

SAR-broh

THE PLANET THEENTOR*

The planet Theentor is a place
Where you do not belong.
You soon discern that something
Is unfathomably wrong.
For anything, at any time,
May vanish into air.
One moment there's a mountain . . .
Seconds later, nothing's there.

Perhaps you see a butterfly,
And then, before you blink,
That butterfly has disappeared—
You don't know what to think.
You're in a grove of stately trees
When suddenly they fade.
You quake with apprehension,
And you're thoroughly dismayed.

On Theentor you experience
Continuous distress,
For everything you're sure is real
Soon turns to nothingness.
The grass on which you rest
Becomes an evanescent mist . . .
And as you try to ponder this,
You simply don't exist.

THEEN-tore

THE WORLD OF THADE[*]

The world of Thade is beautiful,
And seemingly serene,
Replete with trees and lovely blooms
And grass of brilliant green.
You're certain you can breathe the air,
But sadly, you are wrong,
For if you draw a breath on Thade,
Your life does not last long.

The air is thick with particles
No sensor can detect.
In seconds they invade your lungs,
And multiply unchecked.
The evil spreads within you,
And you soon approach your end
In pain too unendurable
To even comprehend.

You have a raging fever,
And a paroxysmal chill,
As in a deep delirium
You writhe against your will.
Your head then swells to twice its size,
You feel a sudden thirst,
Which you don't live to satisfy—
For that is when you burst.

THADE—rhymes with *fade*

The savage monarch of Zazorzz
Reclines upon her throne,
And casually gnaws upon
A broken alien bone.

If you possess so little sense
To venture to Zazorzz,
The bone that she gnaws next upon
Will probably be yours.

zah-ZORZ

THERE IS A SOUND ON NING-FA-DEE *

There is a sound on Ning-fa-dee,
A sound that does not cease,
A sound so loud and piercing
You'll not know a moment's peace.
You cannot run away from it,
It sinks into your brain,
Depriving you of any rest,
And driving you insane.

You race around in anguish,
And you hold your ears for naught.
You fail to shut that sound out,
It consumes your every thought.
You soon begin to scream and scream
In frenzied agony,
And in your pain you perish
On that world called Ning-fa-dee.

NING-fa-DEE

THE STROVILEAN EXPLORERS

The Strovilean explorers
Set their ship down in a field,
Then disembarked the vessel,
Which they carefully concealed.
They'd altered their appearance
So no pair of probing eyes
Could ever hope to penetrate
The shell of their disguise.

The Strovilean explorers
Now continued on their quest,
And soon became disheartened,
Disconcerted, and distressed.
They simply could not fathom
What they could not help but see—
It seemed the world they'd landed on
Was pure catastrophe.

As through that world they wandered,
They were stricken with alarm.
They witnessed its inhabitants
Cause one another harm.
The Strovilean explorers
Were appalled by all they saw—
The unremitting plunder,
And the small regard for law.

There was carnage, chaos, callousness,
Brutality and greed,
Unthinkable indifference
To the plight of those in need.
They saw suffering and hunger
On a scale they'd never faced.
The air was fouled with poisons,
Rivers ran with toxic waste.

Vast legions of combatants
Struggled in a senseless war—
The Strovilean explorers
Could not bear it anymore.
They hastened to their waiting craft
And, safe beneath its dome,
They lifted off from planet Earth,
And sadly headed home.

stroh-VILL-ee-un

Anagram Answers

Drifig = frigid
Fesstor = forests
Gub = bug
Skreber = berserk
Ogdofod = dog food
Sarbro = arbors
Theentor = not there
Thade = death
Ning-fa-dee = deafening

THIS IS A BORZOI BOOK PUBLISHED BY ALFRED A. KNOPF

Text copyright © 2009 by Jack Prelutsky
Illustrations copyright © 2009 by Jimmy Pickering

All rights reserved. Published in the United States by Alfred A. Knopf, an imprint of
Random House Children's Books, a division of Random House, Inc., New York.

Knopf, Borzoi Books, and the colophon are registered trademarks of Random House, Inc.

Visit us on the Web! www.randomhouse.com/kids

Educators and librarians, for a variety of teaching tools, visit us at
www.randomhouse.com/teachers

Library of Congress Cataloging-in-Publication Data
Prelutsky, Jack.
The swamps of Sleethe : poems from beyond the solar system / by Jack Prelutsky ; illustrated by
Jimmy Pickering. — 1st ed.
p. cm.
ISBN 978-0-375-84674-8 (trade) — ISBN 978-0-375-94674-5 (lib. bdg.)
[1. Extrasolar planets—Juvenile poetry. 2. Children's poetry, American.] I. Pickering, Jimmy, ill. II. Title.
PS3566.R36S926 2008
811'.54—dc22
2008006530

The illustrations in this book were created using mixed media.

MANUFACTURED IN CHINA

March 2009

10 9 8 7 6 5 4 3 2 1

First Edition

Random House Children's Books supports the First Amendment and celebrates the right to read.